WHO STARTED THE LABOR DAY CELEBRATION?

Holiday Book for Kids
Children's Holiday Books

BABY PROFESSOR
EDUCATION KIDS

Speedy Publishing LLC

40 E. Main St. #1156

Newark, DE 19711

www.speedypublishing.com

What is Labor Day? It's more than an excuse for a three day weekend and picnic! Let's find out what Labor Day is all about.

CONSTRUCTION TOOLS

HONORING LABOR

What is labor? It is work. People do work of all kinds, for themselves and for others. When people work for other people in exchange for money (so they can buy food for their families and pay the rent), they are called "the workers" or "the labor force". This work does not have to involve a shovel or a mop; computer programmers and skilled medical personnel are also part of the labor force.

The people who hire the workers also do work, but they tend to do work that is safer and cleaner—and pays more. When we talk about "the workers", we usually mean the people who are hired by others, or by the government, to do

all the stuff that makes our civilization possible, from cleaning streets to repairing machines, from picking crops to mining for coal, from assembling trucks to taking care of children in a pre-school.

MAY DAY EVENTS

In the nineteenth century, as nations moved from most work being on farms to most work being in factories, the workers in factories often found they were being paid too little for too much work in dangerous conditions.

WORKERS ON CONSTRUCTION SITE

Workers' associations, and then unions, began to be organized so that the conversation was no longer between the powerful boss and a single unhappy worker, but between the boss and all the workers in the factory.

The boss then had to consider what he would do if the workers went on strike and stopped working. Often it turned out to make sense to increase wages a little or improve working conditions, rather than have the factory sit idle for weeks or months during a strike.

SHIPPING MANAGER AND A WORKER

W orkers wanted the whole community to know what was going on, so community pressure could help convince the owner to negotiate a situation that would let everyone go back to work a little more happy.

Union organizers who hoped for a large change in society, so that owners would have less power and workers would have more, began to hold parades and rallies on May 1 each year. This was known as International Labor Day, and it is still a huge event outside North America.

May 1 was chosen to remember a general strike in Chicago that started May 1, 1886. The goal of the strike was to gain an eight-hour work day for most workers, at a time when owners wanted workers to be in the factory ten or more hours every day, and often on Saturday as well.

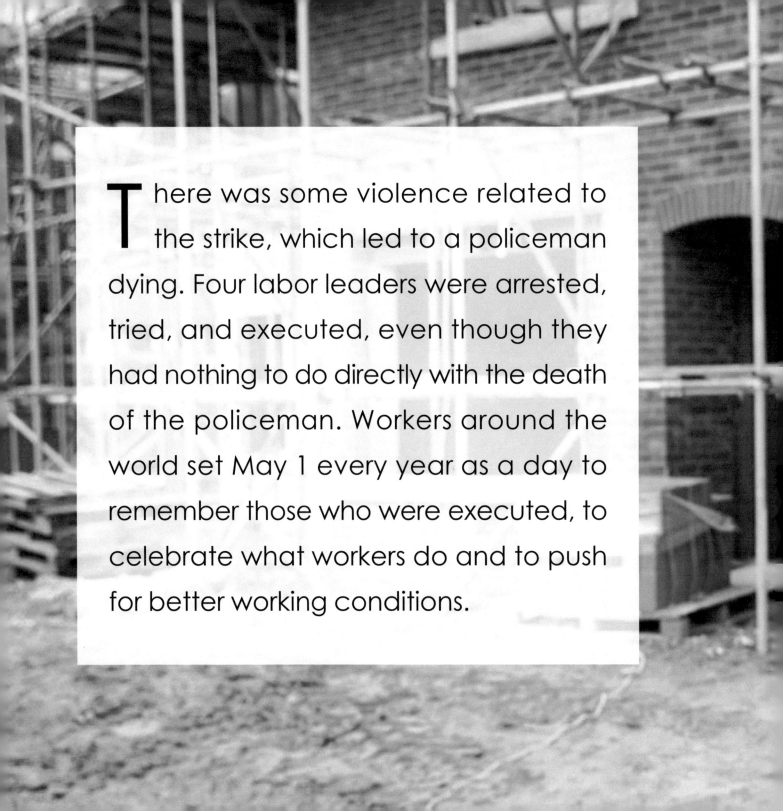

There was some violence related to the strike, which led to a policeman dying. Four labor leaders were arrested, tried, and executed, even though they had nothing to do directly with the death of the policeman. Workers around the world set May 1 every year as a day to remember those who were executed, to celebrate what workers do and to push for better working conditions.

CONSTRUCTION WORKER ON BUILDING SITE

May Day events became important to the labor movement in the United States. Many owners and politicians saw the rising strength of the labor movement as a threat to America's capitalist system, where many laws and traditions supported increasing "capital" (money and other wealth) over other issues like worker health, equal opportunity, or the environment.

In May, 1894, railway workers went on strike and trains could not run. This prevented raw materials from moving to factories and goods from moving from factories to shops. Beyond

this, there was a feeling that perhaps the whole system of powerful owners and struggling workers might change to a system where more people shared both wealth and power.

As part of the resolution of the strike, Democratic President Grover Cleveland declared a national day to honor labor—but not on May 1. May 1 was seen as too much of a symbol of the power of unions. Instead, the politicians settled on the first Monday in September as a national Labor Day, a new holiday.

INDUSTRIAL WORKER CUTTING METAL

MECHANICAL WORKER

THE RISE OF LABOR DAY

In Canada, the Toronto Trades Assembly, a gathering of skilled workers, organized a demonstration to support the rights of workers in 1872. The demonstration called for the release of 24 newspaper workers who were put in jail for going on strike in support of a shorter work day: down to only nine hours!

At this time in Canada, trade unions were illegal and going on strike was seen as a criminal act. But there was great public support for the parade and for the cause of workers. Canada's leaders realized they could not ignore the importance of workers to

the economy. The Canadian government repealed all Canadian laws blocking trade unions, and the Canadian Labour Congress was founded a few years later.

WORKER IN PRODUCTION PLANT

In the United States, September 1 had importance as a worker holiday in several states. Since 1882, some unions in New York and other states had held a celebration on the first Monday in September. This was partly inspired by the demonstrations in Canada. It was a welcome break from long days of work, and a chance to enjoy one more day of good summer weather.

In the late 1800s people regularly worked ten or more hours in factories, got little or no help if they were injured on the job, and had no job security or pension to help them when they could not work any more. On September 5, 1882 more than 10,000 workers left their jobs to march on City Hall in New York to press for enforcement of fair labor laws and for better working conditions. This was the first large-scale labor parade in U.S. history.

BUILDERS LOOKING AT BUILDING PLANS

Many states passed laws recognizing the holiday for working people. Oregon was the first state, in 1887. It was followed by 29 other states before the federal government took action. Finally the U.S. Congress made Labor Day a national holiday in 1894. Selecting the first Monday in September for the holiday, rather than May 1, was an attempt to cause a split between unions that wanted radical change in the economic system and unions that did not.

WORKER WITH PROTECTIVE MASK WELDING METAL

WORKERS COMPENSATION

Applying For A
(Check any that apply)

- [ ] Permit
- [ ] ID Card
- [ ] Renewal
- [ ] Replacement

Identification Information

- Driver license? [ ] Yes [ ] No
- Learner permit? [ ] Yes [ ] No
- Non-driver ID Card? [ ] Yes [ ] No

The objectives will be based on how you gain sales by acquiring and keeping customers. A marketing strategy helps on making good messages with the right twist of marketing approaches in order to have a good outcome of your sales and marketing activities.

Your Personal

Full Last Name

Full First Name   Gender [ ] Male [ ] Female

Date of birth   Day / Month / Year

Nationality

ID card number and Details

enter the identification number it appears on the card

Out-of-State License ID No:

Type of License:

Date of Expiration:

Contact Details

Home Phone

Mobil

Your Personal Details

Eye color

Hight

Email Address: (optional)

Status: [ ] Single [ ] Married [ ] Devorced

Others

Address where you live

Street No.   Street   Post Code

Unit No.   State

Town/City

Address where you live
(This address will appear on your

Has your mailing address change

Other change: What is the chan
(new license cla

Putting your strategy into action is how your marketing plan should work... how you're going to work with your targets, it maybe ...show how your activities to fit your customers buying cycles ...e should be innovativ

(SSN)*   ...ke m

The government action favored the unions that were less militant, and less anxious to change the system of capital and labor under which the United States operates.

WHO THOUGHT OF IT FIRST?

Nobody is quite sure who came up with the idea of Labor Day in the United States. It may have been Peter McGuire, who helped found the American Federation of Labor.

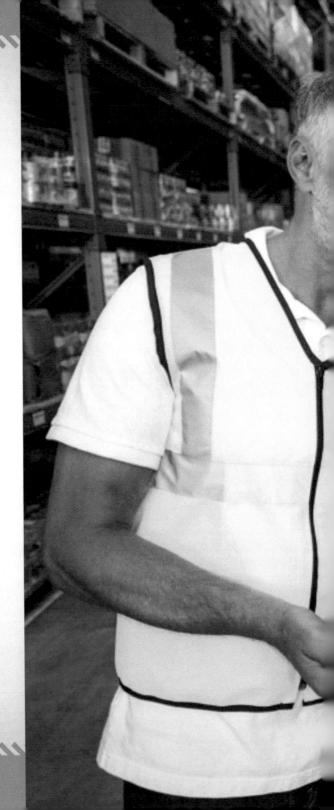

Others say it was another labor leader, Matthew Maguire, who first proposed a holiday for working people. Despite the similarity of their last names, the two men were not related.

WAREHOUSE WORKERS

LABOR DAY TODAY

Through most of the world, May 1, "May Day", is the day to recognize the importance of labor to the world. In the United States, the first Monday in September takes focus.

FEMALE WORKER

Since this holiday gives a three-day weekend at the end of summer and for before the start of the school year, for most families it is a time for some holiday activity rather than marching in support of workers' rights.

Soon after the declaration of the official holiday, even the unions in New York City abandoned their annual parade on the first Monday in September. They felt it could not compete with the attractions of a holiday weekend.

But while it is fun to have a cookout, watch fireworks, or have fun in other ways on Labor Day, it is important not to forget how important working people are to the country.

Here are some things to remember:

- In the 1950s, almost one third of working Americans were in labor unions. That ratio has declined to about 12 percent now, but union labor is still a strong force making possible production in many industries.

- In the United States, there are about 160 million people in the work force. Most of the rest of the population is retired, disabled, too young (under sixteen) to be eligible, in prison, or unavailable for other reasons.

FINANCE TRADE MANAGER WITH BUSINESS CREW

BUSINESSMAN WITH WORKER

- About 60 percent of workers are in "blue collar" jobs. Those are jobs that involve you in physical work that is often dirty and sometimes risky.

- The most common jobs in the U.S. are:

  o Salespeople in stores (4.6 million)

  o Cashiers (3.4 million)

  o Food service workers (3.1 million)

  o Clerks in offices (2.9 million)

  o Registered nurses (2.7 million)

  o Customer service representatives (2.5 million)

  o Waiters and waitresses (2.4 million)

  o Laborers and people who move and transport freight and raw materials (2.4 million)

BUSINESS COLLEAGUES WORKING

A HAPPY WORKPLACE

- A work area that is growing very quickly is personal care aides. These people help older and less-able people, especially the elderly, be safe, healthy and active.

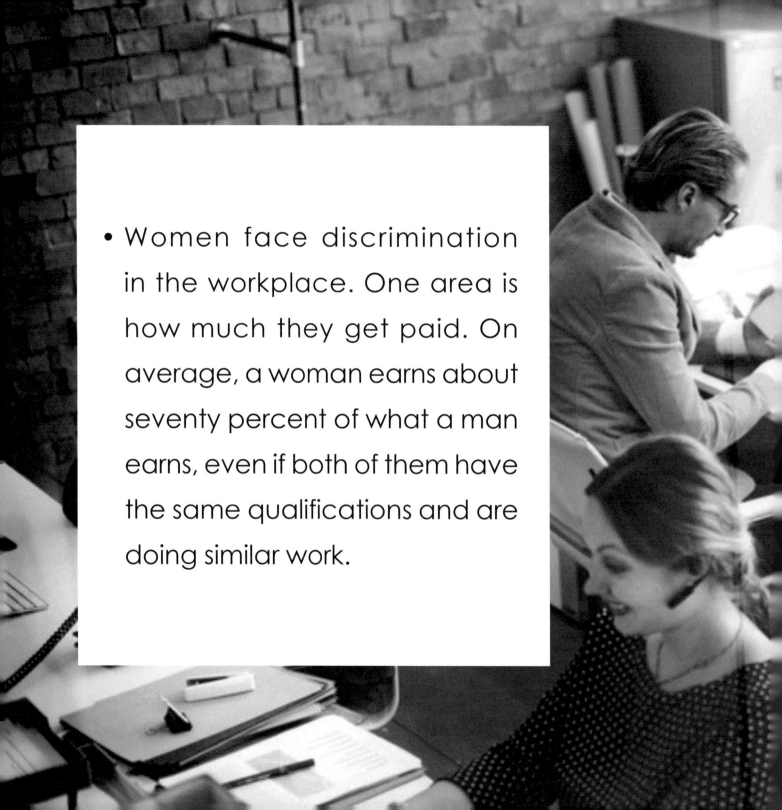

- Women face discrimination in the workplace. One area is how much they get paid. On average, a woman earns about seventy percent of what a man earns, even if both of them have the same qualifications and are doing similar work.

OFFICE WORKERS

WORKERS UNITED

Working people get together to negotiate for fairer wages, for better working conditions, and for other benefits. A lot of things we take for granted, like not working on the weekend, are a result of the efforts of labor unions. Learn more in the Baby Professor book The Beginnings of the Labor Unions.